Of Algae & Grief
Pip Osmond-Williams

Winner of the 2021 Brian Dempsey Memorial Competition

Of Algae and Grief

© Pip Osmond-Williams

First Edition 2021

Pip Osmond-Williams has asserted her authorship and given permission to Dempsey & Windle for these poems to be published here.

All rights reserved. No part of this publication may be reproduced, stored in a retrieval system or transmitted in any form or by any means without the written consent of the author, nor otherwise circulated in any form of binding or cover other than that in which it is published and without a similar condition being imposed on a subsequent purchaser.

Published by Dempsey & Windle

15 Rosetrees
Guildford
Surrey
GU1 2HS
UK
01483 571164
dempseyandwindle.com

A catalogue record for this book is available from the British Library

British Library Cataloguing-in-Publication Data

ISBN: 978-1-913329-62-4

Printed and bound in the UK

For Jane, as always

Contents

Girlsong	5
Cartography	6
Cianalas	7
Yesnaby	8
Rockpooling	10
After the Tumour	11
Colony	12
Heirloom	13
Lucretia	14
Harvest	15
Tantalion Road	16
Levenwick Beach	17
Medusa	18
Brown Shrimp	19
Teneu	20
Pollux	22
Migration	23
The Amazon Woman	24
Father	26
Primogeniture	27
The Salters' Way	28
Metamorphosis	29
Midas	30
Maids	31
Optic Tricks	32
Winter Solstice, 2020	33
Life Cycle	34
Acknowledgements	35
About the Author	36

Girlsong

you say I can't keep doing this
                                      that somebody found me
trying to swim with the mute swans again
                   telling them about the scythe-winged swifts
                             & bone-pin whitethroats
how the migratory birds outfly me when I call
                            you say that in the water
somebody found me measuring the lengths
of all I love in knots   of sweet galingale
that when the wardens came
my arms & hands were cottongrass &
               from the side it looked as though my mouth
                       was speckled blue & O
a song thrush egg or a scream
       through which I try to heave the lilies from my throat
& somehow come up empty
               you say that when they finally slipped me
from my raincoat & freshwater hoops
of algae & grief
                   I kept talking about monotypic species
      about white rings pooled around Lir
about how I must call my mother

Cartography

The MRI reveals a map. He won't say
if it's moons or mountains,
but there are abnormalities
then absent space.
He points to the couloir, her collapse,
sheer cliff walls stretching out from
otherwise solid mass, or a small-scale
lunar graben – he calls it *intrusive
volcanism*. For months I scrub
at the stain beneath the stairs.
The tumour, he says, is a massif or
the serenity sea, pink evening eclipse
in the harp of the skull. It's either
alpine carcinoma or stellar metastasis,
but we never find out. They cut her open
and I go home, roll rock formations
around my mouth like stones
from a plum. In the ICU
he is charting astrocytes against
the northern hemisphere, Ursa Major
from coast to coast. When we speak
again, hushed voices about
the limits of human endurance,
I am picturing her waving a flag
from the equinox, deserving more
than what the earth gave up.

Cianalas

Your breath starts to taste of salt and meadowsweet, wine bruises the colours of northern marsh orchids, and Stroma moves inside you when you speak. My body is divided into straths and crofts and lochs, you call me Angelica in your sleep, and I'm left to wonder if skin can develop features of the sea. From a tenement block each night you swim out to the Pentland Firth. You wake me early, let me unravel kelp from wrists and ligaments. I carry your secret: blue rings kept tightly bound around your heart and feet.

Yesnaby

I am trying to offer you
something in return for Iolaire

or these splintered crags
flagstones of salt-blood and tar

your body in a shorefront bothy
the sweet half moon rising

and falling beside herself
above soft lines of the land

I am trying to peel myths and witches
from my milk-thin throat to give to you

the sea-lashed boy
but each time I falter

on unspoken words of the Sea Mither
old love that left on the southward equinox

pushing this slip disc heart of mine away
I proclaim that folklore's a fool's game

bring me the puckered lips of cowrie shells
the unsung joys of beachcombing

primula scotica kissing our streaming feet
corncrake calls on coarse wind

distant Caithness and these open palms
coffee-soaked breath on a damp cheek

easy with you to sift silver from salt
know this but still forgive me

if I mistake sea stacks for Finfolk fingers
an oystercatcher's wing for Hildaland

sea mist for gas rings I would stand beside
with her when I was a girl

some days some clouds linger
flotsam jetsam lagan and derelict

Rockpooling

At the shore swell of Kinnagoe Bay,
in between abandonment and faultline return,
his pale face sleeps in the sea bowls –
hair now bladderwrack, pulmonary disease
a jellyfish, silver-webbed and floating.
Curled between the spines of a stickleback
are our years, blue and sweet,
but when I try to scoop
what remains of us from small waters,
fulmars swoop for me
like a mother,
believe me intertidal
when in the water I am
all father, the sea-dark soft beached body,
pieced together from whale bone and iron lung.
It doesn't sing, spills instead its strange hymns
into the salt bloom of the undertow,
blood rush between the heart's cathedral chambers.
Some nights it leaves to the sand a heavy skin
of lamentation, old tidal marks of water loss.
Sometimes the body is just cavity
to crawl between, moor beneath,
hands stretched out to bronchi of myth and fog.

After the Tumour

when you say progress / what you mean is / the only salted thing's the aubergine / when you say take stock / what you mean is / a party trick: / balancing eggs in the perfect jaws of strangers / when you say obscene / what you mean is / bitter as the cud / and when you say magnanimous / what you mean is / elusive fathers / struck dumb on pedestals // when you say longing / what you mean is / the sample taken from the lake / the town council awaits results / when you say empathic / what you mean is / searching out your mother's shape / in clouds and CT scans / when you say coherence / what you mean is / have you / banged your head / and when you say an ending / what you mean is / sincerely yours / as ever // when you say the aftermath / what you mean is / no dipping toes in water / thicker than blood is metastasis / when you say take heart / what you mean is / your offer of a heavy one / when you say bad faith / what you mean is / the sullied god as sweet relief / and when you say relief / what you mean is / Peggy in the garden by the hollyhocks / talking in lines / instead of circles

Colony

The birds outside the window do not
know that you're gone. Like eggs

we've stayed indoors for days, cradling grief
as a moon in our arms who refuses to eat with us

at the table. She doesn't sleep, so it's early
when I dress myself in something like a Sunday

best, take baby steps outside. A flash of blue,
something blue. Air gathers in a cotton well

upon my tongue. Time's unstitched from
my throat their names you knew, but they

live in my body like a harp. My hands are all
stale bread and sour milk. I look to the birds

but for what? What is it that holds their hymns
and wings aloft? Silence splits the lip

and in a bloody rush I say I am with you in
this time of sorrow. Hands in dripping mouth

I say I am so sorry for your loss. They take
three steps back, stare blankly from the holly bush.

Heirloom

I started smoking cigarettes
on my father's knee aged three
the glowing ends curling around
our heads and the television set
as we watched the races
on a Saturday
the light of his eyes
pale as the dome
of a midsummer sky
his gold ashtray piled high
with the chalk dead ends
of Lucky Strikes
and me, a smudge of a girl,
my hair still gold and light
chasing those silver ringlets
with my stubby chubby fingers
he would waft them away
not see my longing for the
dragons around my head
and then he would
take another drag again

Lucretia

I found you one night with Susanna's milk
                         smeared around your mouth
blinking under our hall light
                         in a slip dress newly split
you began to weave your hair with laurel seeds
                         and stopped eating at the table
you said you couldn't bear the thought
of pulped flesh   offered pink in scallop shells
honey drip from sticky fingers   spoilt cream
touching clagging grease   at the bottom of the pan

some mornings I would wake to find you
                         naked in the garden
threading your body with pine needles
            pinning scorched damselflies to your chest
fearful that the earth would abandon you
                        before you could abandon it
                you would not let me touch you
and in the half-light you cursed the moon
                   for the pear drops of your skin
the blackberry kiss of your swollen tongue
           how it felt to feed him
in an uncertain spring
            the silver birch clung to your dawn chorus
that you sung blindly into the wind
                   against my will I will leave you

                         after you were gone
I planted pomegranate seeds into the bowls
of the earth that you had left

that summer
              all I could dream about were orange groves

Harvest

You think you saw a murder in the gloaming,
corvids teaching their young the hunger
in the dying, so you bring to me our last harvest.
Let me learn patience watching you
unpeel jam jars sticky with fruit,
a sloe bloom that turns our thighs to bruises,
berry wine, tart and cool, slipping
neatly down the throat.
You take out the final, holy glory:
a bowl of plums, almost fit to bursting.
See how they yield at light pressure?
We devour their soft flesh slowly,
knowing that when you have licked my wrists
blue-clean of juice, the stones no longer
pitted with our blood, you will leave me
digging dirt beneath paling thrift and sheep's sorrel.
The last of the summer, you and your black pinions,
wing-flight making light of flesh and bone again.

Tantallon Road

When you try to leave me
in the morning
apologetically
I trace the ring of Apollo
around my finger
the Mount of Venus
where you kissed me coarse
and sweet in the dark
then my arm
the crescent of my ear and eyelid
the flush of my hips and then
back to my palm.
If I stretch for you
in your good blue suit
it's only because I want to tell you
that I know you've heard me pray
sweet Jesus
for temperate days
but in the dawning of
your muted room
I would rather you
melt me on your tongue
like a sugar cube
sweat like manuka honey
dripping from the spoon.
Come bury yourself as cutlery
in the crook of me.
It's still early
you could just close the door
and leave the coffee.

Levenwick Beach

The land lies soft enough for a burial
and the wind reprieves blown sand white-brittle as bone
and the haar bears down, caging the sky in half-breath
to keep her from spilling the unsayable
about the days that slip right out of our hands.
Here you stand, ahead of me, trying to skip stones
at the pulse of the shore. Love, tell me how
your good flesh lacks the cold sea fret, or
how to trawl a bed, expose neither driftwood
nor ghost net but find the mainsail and rope,
the chart and bridle, the black calm before the swell.

Medusa

You didn't always hate the sea.

In another time,
by the shores of Sarpedon
you would dip your hardened heels
and threads of rust and gold in blue,
wave to Selene as she looked down upon
the girls burning coils of citronella
by the waters of Cisthene beach.
In another time,
you and Euryale collected seaweed and shells
(a strand for every man who looks your way,
a cephalopod for every heart you think you'll break)
popped olives in your blistering mouths like cherries,
kissing the scrapes on each other's hands
like you did when you were girls.
In another time,
you were scared of the snakes who hissed in the dunes.
I should have told you to be scared instead
of the monsters inside the temple,
the sea and its thunderous pools.
For you, Medusa, I will never speak his name.
Do not listen when she tells you
that you are more losing battle than gentle girl.
She weaves salt in the wounds of divinity's war
then waits to watch the women burn.

The owl swoops and claws
at the roots of your hair and skin.
banshee whore harlot gorgon
m o n s t e r

you, Medusa, who could not swim.

Brown Shrimp

when she speaks of
reorienting herself as sea lavender,
taking small consolation in her salt-bitten body
clustered pretty and stiff,
we're back in high school biology class,
being taught the art of camouflage
as protection, admiration for the burrowing demeanour
of *crangon crangon*, behavioural plasticity
and environmental adaptation

in quiet rooms, I appraise my thighs as moon jellyfish
their common sink into the seabed, neither sting
nor swim, only soft shallow lapse
in wait for the tide to reject them

we are told the ocean in its sweetest moments
is the ripe weight of our names in the nets the men cast

their sky our limit // the blue archive of longing

Teneu

On the shivering edge of Traprain Law,
I begged him to push me.
I pleaded with the cliffs
to offer me their salvation,
make me weightless,
let me become again
a part of the earth and sea from which I came.
The gannets and kittiwakes can take me,
or just let me wake up hidden
within the silk-water skin
of a selkie. By starlight and peat flame,
I wanted to be shrouded in the mist
that would make me legend,
a whisper, untraceable.
Rather that than have them ever
touch me again.

In water,
even the slough of a snake
bears a heavy weight,
but on willow rods I took to floating.
Endless days I spent,
cast under the swell of the Sea Mither,
unfolding the length of myself
to the cacophonic call of gulls.
In blood-soaked evenings of the Aurora,
I heard the battle cries
of my sisters in the wind,
and I dreamed about tsunamis,
the end of things,
the underbelly of an elephant.

From Lavellan depths I finally
forced myself from the Firth,
dug my nails in the gasping land
and grasped the hand of Serf,
the crutch of him,
who whispered old Orcadian psalms
into my burning, bleeding ears,
and with a burr I felt you breathing.
Then my skin was not theirs but mine again,
how I swam into the caves of it,
reaching a throne of peach and blood
in the seat of which a baby slept.

In Cathures,
by the banks of the Clyde,
I think often of the looms of time,
the black moon seed
and the rocks that cradled me,
the jagged edge that made me again
half ocean, half sky.
From my sheltered breast,
you fix your tiny eyes on Traprain Law
ablaze in kerosene.
One day, I'll sing you
a lullaby of a clifftop and a mother:
empty furrows, I'll croon to you,
where the water once ran to save me.

Pollux

You, my brother of summer,
tell us around the table that autumn berries
are your favourite fruit. You like the way
they taste sweeter with the bruising.
If I could, I would take from the old house
the last of the crop. I would pound
their pound of purple flesh for you.
I would bring you the ravens,
the mortar and bricks.
Do you remember when our hair
was long and we only had one mouth?
Do you remember how we'd lap
pity like milk from human hands?

Migration

That first summer,
we mistook their bodies
for shrapnel. The second,
their wings for a shiv.
We lost faith in flight,
forgot to seek hope in
the shape of a bird, calling
our names from the prayer wall
to the west coast   swift and fleeting
We let slip what it's like to come home again,
somehow fear it. A test, of course –
      that year, the earth bound our bodies
quietly to its own   we did not feel it
but salt blood became seafoam
          murmuring wet lines
of swell and retreat
      the windows were open
something returned, brown-bellied,
      in a frenzy and drift
it looked like survival
or celestial cue
      it sounded like wings drumming
          in the north of the house

The Amazon Woman

There is silence on these islands now,
save for the skua call. Brief are the days
and still I miss the parliament,
harsh soil taunted by the lore of trees,
blood yolk of the gannet's bed,
salt spill from the puffin kill,
the rancid stench of flesh in cleits.
All the blind and gut reminders
of a life, lives, what it is
to be still living.

In purple mornings
with earth's funeral smoke
curling up the crags of Boreray,
I picture barefoot circles of blackhouse girls,
their linen dresses stitched with blood,
running from the moon-mouthed boys,
split lips licked in mustard and salt.
Sometimes I follow them, try to tuck
their splintered skin into the
curves and folds of Gleann Mor,
try to warn them of the smaller wars –
of love lodged under the scalloped edge,
mother tongues in the mouths of caves,
loss breathing life into different shapes:
the bell curve of a diving bird,
the space of the wave between.
There are places that I will never know.
They left with backs and shoulders
of flint and stone on the Harebell
away from Oiseval.

I use my time wisely now.
I pluck honeysuckle from rocks
to learn about exposure.
I have found new ways
to tolerate salt.
I think of them often, often.
Some nights I wake, believing that I
have only dreamed this mountain still.
Skua take flight, diving in ribbons
through the sky's white line,
the scavenge for wreckage
for forgotten life, some small secular
devotion to the day, another day.

Father

You remember he learned at the altar
salvation pooled in a gold half cup, sadness
licked clean from fingers of meala. Your soft light
splits—O crowman, dolmen,
dead man back from the oíche.

He unveils a rookery in his liver the birds
have been making out of your favourite clothes;
a canary he keeps in a cage (polydipsia-struck
but christ, how you fall for its fair fragile hymn);
his hope to rewild in a vineyard the self, its sweetest
pieces: vitis vinifera blood, salt-pillared skin,
the flesh-pulped, pithy heart.

You never know what to do when he's like this.
You recall the news you heard: the swallows
may never return to the Mission San Juan Capistrano.
He kisses a stained glass lip and refuses the eye.
Rose light shifts and some memory stirs
of small eaves abandoned in sanctified land.

He says he wants to stay but he never does.
Somewhere outside, a nightjar churrs; inside,
two hands tremble. A small heart adjures
in the caged bird's aching throat.
In the morning you remember
its pitiful, immeasurable thirst.

Primogeniture

From the sunken dell
      of my brother's throat
            we're trying to recover
                  what is left of our mother.
          If not the alveolar tap
     then maybe its oval
shape, if not the trap–
      bath then maybe the
            foot–strut split. If not
                the words then the song and
         if not the song then the
     lips and if not the lips
then the tongue that taps
      and licks the cigarette
           from which the apple
                falls to the earth. In cephalic
          veins we find evidence
    of a burial. I stand small
against the years, the bees
      having been in his body
           for so long his arms start
                leaking honey. With liminal
            lines between them, those
      lugworm casts of the skin,
I chart his face, her gold
      shape. When he speaks
           again, he is singing the echo
                part of a song for which we
           have never had a name
      know only as ours

The Salters' Way

I keep dreaming of Jenkin Chapel
in green and brown and gold,
standing by you as you called
the lapwing evensong
into the twilight like a preacher.
You seemed as from the earth
as the limestone on which we climbed.
With squinted brow you searched
for the crest of the vanellus, a flicker
of black and white among the honey,
the song of the northern bird.
Nesh to the bone,
for the call of the green plover
you withstood the cold.
Sometimes, somewhere from
the sky behind (I still think of you
as where the peach and gold would meet)
we would hear them, singing from
the sodden dirt, shrieking back
to their north-west sisters,
pack horses laden with the salt
of the Cheshire witches
peewit, peewit
your hands grasping the drystone walls
you always said would outlast us all.
I thought of you as kin of the fields
through which the lapwing flew –
of Windgather Rocks,
Shutlingsloe's peak, the moon you
had me believe was made for me.
By Jenkin Chapel, I made that
age-old mistake of imagining
you to be ageless.

Metamorphosis

A girl wakes to find her body replaced
by a guillemot egg, her room now
the vast screaming sky of a cliff edge.
Does she miss the dark slip of the girl
she had been – her tender mouth,
androgynous hips – or does she
breathe in this bed of salt
and gold and absence,
hold out two wings to one
brief and glorious life.
Picture this: the girl hatching,
unable to fly yet born ready
in primitive parachute. At her skyline
is Caithness. Below her father
is helmsman in a dress of green kelp,
shouting her down to the sea.
When she jumps, she hears the waves
crashing in the key of her name.

Midas

in his garden we would count the colours
pink lemonade, sweetbriar rose, the flesh of a cantaloupe

every time I fall in love, I see my father's hands dripping butter-
scotch and boysenberry into the blind-baked and sweetened earth

before gold, before the finch became the eagle, before the wool
became the fleece, before the tremors begging sweating clawing

we practised father-daughter dances among the wildflowers
shoulder to shoulder, palm to palm, then cheek to cheek

the doctor gives him pills for the pain, saltwater for the ache
but christ I know the craving keeps a different clock

within the doll of him there's another one, another
one, another and he pulls out their hair with shaking hands

he only knows love as lingering, longing as tangible
father, father, let me weave you a dress of thirst and grief:

you will know loss sitting in the citadel spinning silk
from particles, threading webs of gold that only you can touch

Maids

He was not the first
man we met on the salt path,
heavy, heavy with the grief of the sea.
The nights would lengthen in light, pink
and gold of a baby's palm, and still from
cracked ribs of rowing boats they'd come,
pebbledash ghosts bound at the wrists
by the days. Over the seawall
they would reach for us:
how hard can it be,
floating?
Not once did they
ask about our blue arms,
our hibiscus lungs, the brine and
ire we keep steeped in the teeth and
throat. There's only so much you can do
for a man who will be dead by morning.
Let us turn out the fog lights, call last
orders, watch him stagger the path
to a tide-marked woman, tired
of the earth and the clay.

Optic Tricks

We left her in the Pennines among the sandpipers
and the woodsmoke, the small flecks taking root
beneath Norway spruce and the sickener.
We raised a beer at the top, took the long way home.
I know this and yet there's this small business
of finding her still in the most unusual places:
in the flight patterns of starlings,
the bright yellow days my brother slices
and quarters, in soft clementine peel rotting
with seed, the laybys before and after the hospital,
in seabirds that dive beneath the in-between,
or the dog that barks after the car has gone,
then with my tongue tasting blood
at the backs of my teeth.
It's not always like this. Sometimes I think I see her
in front of me, waiting for the traffic lights.

Winter Solstice, 2020

after the smokestacks / after they stood in their wild silence watching buildings burning through the long dark half / after a bidding war erupted / for scrubland three parts fire one part song / after they told us to stand tall shoulder on keep breathing / normally / after the party / the after party / their dance to planes they never hear / now that they live under the flight path / after the last time / after the / last / time after / time / last time after / time after time / the last //

                                        still, you wake dreaming
of marsh samphire creeping
                        through the fronds of your palm
lemon verbena   at the foot of the bed
some things stay green in the heart
        some days we make the best of our bad lot
              when the roads thaw we'll leave the city
                      I'll kiss you beneath Cìr Mhòr again
lick rock salt from the spindrift
become lugworm soft   and split
                from a sea-wracked duneshell body
tremble the brief and silent promise
                        lighter days are coming

Life Cycle

When I go home, if I go home, I will
lick and stitch the skylark's silver songline
into my skin, cup the full-fat belly
sticky sweet with slips and gorse, come back to
you again. When I go home, if I go
home, there in the lime and smoke I will wrap
half-rhyme around alder trees, old man swamp-
dweller, all catkins and leather, shifting
me out to the east. When I go home, if
I go home, to the mayflies I will teach
secrets in leaving indelible marks,
how I think of you in lunar phases,
the waning crescent or the waxing heart.
When I go home, if I go home, I will
bury my dead in her alkaline soil –
undress in the dark, let her down gently,
come back to you again.

Acknowledgments:

I am grateful to the editors of the following journals and anthologies in which some of the poems from this collection were first published: 'Heirloom' and 'Medusa' in *From Glasgow to Saturn*; 'Tantallon Road' in *New Writing Scotland* (ASLS, 2019); 'Teneu' in *Island and Sea* (Scottish Writers' Centre, 2020); 'The Amazon Woman' in *Northwords Now*, 'Cianalas', 'Yesnaby' and 'Life Cycle' in *Channel*, 'Midas' in *Poetry Scotland*; 'Girlsong', 'Colony' and 'After the Tumour' in *Horses of a Different Colour* (Dempsey & Windle, 2021); 'Lucretia' and 'Winter Solstice 2020' in *Gutter*.

My heartfelt thanks to my publishers, Dempsey & Windle, and Callum James for their belief in this collection when it was still in its infancy, and my friends and family – in particular Gilly, Naomi and Will – for their undiluted enthusiasm and support. A special thank you to Jim, my wonderful brother, and Stuart, my beloved heart, for all your encouragement over the past few years – I love you both endlessly.

About the Author

Pip Osmond-Williams grew up in the north of England and moved to Glasgow in 2010, where she is still based. She holds a PhD in Scottish Literature from the University of Glasgow and works as an editorial assistant and academic researcher. In 2020, she was shortlisted for the Alastair Reid Pamphlet Prize at the Wigtown Poetry Festival. Her poems have been published in the UK and Ireland.

Pip Osmond-Williams' debut pamphlet, *Of Algae & Grief*, features poems from her winning entry to the Brian Dempsey Memorial Competition in 2021. Combining the personal and the mythological, much of the collection examines grief – in its various forms and stages – through the lens of nature, exposing the ways in which the absence of a person can punctuate the living world. Real and imagined bodies of water permeate *Of Algae & Grief*, providing spaces through which to explore the swell and return of loss, love and hope.